SELLING YOUR HOME IN SEATTLE

100 Lessons to Maximize the Results of Your Sale

Kim Pelham

Published by Pacelli Publishing
Bellevue, Washington

SIX
~WORD
LESSONS

Six-Word Lessons on Selling Your Home in Seattle

All rights reserved. No part of this book may be reproduced or transmitted in any form or by any means, electronic or mechanical including photocopying, recording or by any information storage or retrieval system, without the written permission of the publisher, except where permitted by law.

Limit of Liability: While the author and the publisher have used their best efforts in preparing this book, they make no representation or warranties with respect to accuracy or completeness of the content of this book. The advice and strategies contained herein may not be suitable for your situation. Consult with a professional when appropriate.

Copyright © 2017 by Kim Pelham

Published by Pacelli Publishing
9905 Lake Washington Blvd. NE, #D-103
Bellevue, Washington 98004
PacelliPublishing.com

Cover and interior designed by Pacelli Publishing
Author photo by Amelia Soper
Cover image by Will Flanagan
Photos on linked pages by Will Flanagan and Sarah Vanasudoll

ISBN-10: 1-933750-71-5
ISBN-13: 978-1-933750-71-2

Table of Contents

Introduction 5

Testimonials 8

Dedication 10

To Move or Not to Move? 11

Seattle-ish Things that Can Influence Price 23

Selecting a Broker to Represent You 33

Getting Your Home Ready to Sell 45

Staging to Increase Your Bottom Line 57

Neutralizing Negatives or Converting to Positives ... 67

My Top 10 Pointers for Staging 79

Just Before and First Week Listed 91

Sale Timeline One: Pending through Appraisal 103

Sale Timeline Two: the Last Week 117

Acknowledgments 127

Introduction

A Shocking Story

I was at a networking event and mentioned that I had just completed a book on how to sell your house in Seattle. Another real estate broker in the group snorted and said, "That's easy! Just stick a sign in the front yard!"

This is the attitude that many real estate brokers and home owners have—that it doesn't take much to sell a house in this hot marketplace. Ah, but the question is how do you maximize the sale? How do you know that you are not leaving tens of thousands of dollars on the table?

Recently, I came across a listing that told a shocking story of missed opportunity and money left behind.

It was a beautiful home in a highly desirable, West Seattle neighborhood—more than 2,000 square feet with fantastic views, a gorgeous granite kitchen and a fabulous his-and-hers master bath, plus a legal apartment in the basement. It was originally priced at $549,000, sold for $532,500 and was listed with two bedrooms (although tax records show three bedrooms). The main photo shows a tiny house with a one car garage. If you had the patience to scroll all the way to the very end, picture #25 shows that the back side of the house is three stories tall with floor-to-ceiling bay windows and sweeping views.

I was shocked because this house should have sold for $630,000 to $650,000 minimum. The problem was that it was marketed poorly and had been listed incorrectly, making it virtually invisible on the Internet.

It is sad because the sellers are probably feeling pretty good right now, thinking they saved two percent on commissions by listing with a well-known discount brokerage. They have no idea that this $10,650 discount actually cost them more than $100,000.

Sadly, I see this kind of thing regularly. I wrote this book because it drives me crazy to see unprofessional listings and missed opportunities. I passionately believe that every seller has the right to receive expert advice and excellent service, whether their home is waterfront property worth millions or a $175,000 condo in Everett.

The 100 lessons in this book are designed to maximize the sale of your home and make sure that you are not leaving money on the table. I hope you enjoy this book and find the information useful. If you have any questions or comments, please feel free to contact me via email at Kim@ThePelhamGroupNW.com or by phone at 425-213-8761.

A Note About the Internet Links:

In several places in this book, I have inserted links to supplemental material and photos on my website that show examples of the principles being discussed. I am committed to maintaining these links, and if you find that a link is broken, please email me, and we will get it fixed ASAP! Thank you.

Go to ThePelhamGroupNW.com/photo-gallery for a summary page of links used throughout the book.

Testimonials

Kim gave me sound advice and worked tirelessly to help me transform my house. Kim and I worked together to increase my home's value by 39 percent. We had 19 offers, and sold for $25,000 over list price.
--Rick Marshall

When our condo didn't sell after two months on the market, we fired our broker and hired Kim. She is very detail-oriented with great instincts for staging and decorating. Kim expertly staged our condo, and it sold in one week for $5,000 more than previously listed. We cannot recommend Kim enough as a listing agent.
--Hui Sun and Nick Ingerson

Kim's expert staging presented my house in the best light possible WITHOUT having to invest in new interior paint and carpet. I got multiple offers and sold in just six days for $22,000 over list price. -- Karen Harley

I chose Kim as my agent after meeting with her because she is not only willing to go the extra mile for her clients but knew the importance of presentation, right down to the signage. She staged my house beautifully, turning it into a showcase "model" home, and helped me with a strategy that ended up selling my house in 5 days for $31,000 over the list price. I would definitely work with Kim again. –Lisa Robinson

Kim is well connected to a wide network of professionals in many fields and has previous experience in construction and business, which adds to the depth of her expertise in real estate. She understands the market, works very hard for her clients, communicates clearly, and responds quickly. She is one of the nicest people I have met since moving to this area and I feel like we gained a real friend by working with her. My husband and I give Kim our highest recommendation. –Stephanie Rothermel

Dedication

When I received the message that *Six-Word Lessons* had selected me to write this book, I was flattered and excited—but also very worried that I was too busy to get it done in the required time frame. I almost said no. This book is dedicated to Brien Pelham, my husband of 34 years, who insisted that I jump on this opportunity and then encouraged me throughout the process. This book wouldn't have been written without him.

Thank you for all your support through the years. Love you. 😊

To Move or Not to Move?

1

This book is not about buying.

BUT where will you go once you sell your house? You must have a plan and feel confident that you can make the change or you will never be able to pull the trigger and decide to sell your existing house.

What does a "balanced market" mean?

When there is an even number of buyers and sellers, we call this a "balanced market." In a balanced market, there would be enough inventory to last about six months if no new houses were listed. In recent years, we have been running with one to two months of inventory in the Seattle area, resulting in a severe housing shortage.

Why Seattle has a housing shortage

People hesitate to list their homes because they don't feel confident they will be able to buy their next home, which then becomes a vicious cycle. In January 2017, Realtor.com rated Seattle the #1 top market feeling the housing crunch. This is because of a flow of foreign money, investment firms buying up rentals and apartments, and an influx of tech workers.

4

Your listing broker needs buying strategies.

When you are interviewing brokers to sell your home, you are also selecting the person who will help you win or lose when you buy your next house. Ask about their multiple offer strategies and success rate with buyers. This is crucial. You need someone with a plan who can WIN your next home in this market!

5

It's a good time to upsize.

At higher price points, fewer buyers qualify to purchase so there is less competition and more availability with higher-priced or luxury homes. Plus, our historically low interest rates increase your buying power and help keep your payments lower. (See Lesson 9 on Interest Rates.)

Buying the next house on contingency?

Buying your next home contingent on the sale of your existing home can be difficult to impossible, especially in certain neighborhoods—but it does happen occasionally. It is easier to accomplish if you are selling a starter home and moving up into a luxury home or if the new home is in an outlying area. It is also easier if you are buying in the fall or winter.

7

The real estate market is cyclical.

The price of real estate goes up and down, with the overall cycle historically being eighteen years, and the up phases lasting seven to ten years. The last peak was in 2006, and the crash was in 2008. No one knows for sure when the next downturn will come—but it is certain that prices will not go up forever. Go to bit.ly/REcycles for an in-depth article on real estate cycles.

The real estate market is seasonal.

Both buyer demand and home prices are highest in the spring, although in recent years, the upswing has started as early as January. Demand and prices both usually remain strong through June. Typically, we see a slump at the end of summer going into fall where competition wanes and prices drop a bit. Then, volume decreases even more during the holiday months.

Low interest rates are VERY important!

Every one percent increase in interest rates decreases buying power by ten percent! So, selling your home when the rates are low makes sense because there are more buyers available for your current home, plus it will be easier to buy your next home. Keep an eye on interest rates. If they start to go up, our hot market may cool down.

10

What are YOUR reasons to sell?

Are you getting older and want to sell the big house and buy nice rambler or a condo with no yard maintenance? Will you be taking care of Mom and Dad and want them to have their own space with a mother-in-law unit? Or, perhaps your family is growing. Only you can make the decision that it is time to make a change and move on in your life.

Seattle-ish Things that Can Influence Price

11

Parking can affect your home's value.

While Uber and Lyft have made it more convenient to live without a car, we are a community of commuters, and parking availability affects your home's value. A secured, underground parking space may be worth $20,000 to $50,000 in downtown Seattle and $10,000 to $20,000 in the suburbs.

How much for views or waterfront?

Sound, lake, mountain, city, golf course—these are just a few of the thirteen different types of views, and there are seventeen different types of waterfront. Each view and waterfront property needs an independent evaluation, based on the type, amount of obstruction, availability of moorage, etc. Interestingly, one study found an unobstructed view of the Puget Sound in a downtown condo building increased value by eighteen percent.

Studies for landslide and geotech issues

Living on a hill or bluff may give you a fantastic view, but it comes with the possibility of landslide. If there is any indication of soil problems with your property, get in front of the issue by having the geotech studies done in advance and making them available to buyers.

14

Why your home's Walk Score matters.

Walkscore.com rates your home's walkability based on its proximity to transit and the number of services that can be accessed without a car. A score of 90 or more is a walker's paradise. In 2014 through 2016, an increase of just one point in a Walk Score added almost one percent to a home's total value.

15

Your home's school rating is important.

Greatschools.org gives every school a ranking on a scale of 1 to 10. This tool is popular with buyers because it helps them quickly determine the quality of the schools. A higher Schools Rating will increase the value of your home and help it sell faster too.

16

Know the value of your zoning.

A duplex may be currently worth $1.4 million, but if it has LR-3 zoning, the value of the property could be doubled by tearing it down and building four condos worth $600-$700K each. Any zoning other than straight-residential should be evaluated for "scrape-and-build" potential and then marketed accordingly.

Investors often love Urban Village Zoning.

Urban Villages were implemented in 1994 to create an experience where people can walk to transit, restaurants, stores and other services. This zoning is appealing to investors and developers because it allows for higher density housing and has greatly diminished requirements for the minimum number of parking spaces per house.

18

Floating homes are cool but rare!

There is nothing more Seattle-ish than the iconic floating homes in Lake Union and Portage Bay. These are listed in the Multiple Listing Service along with regular real estate, and they are rare indeed! For example, at the time of writing, there were 1,138 active listings in the city of Seattle; six of these were floating homes and two were houseboats. There were only thirty-one floating home and houseboat sales in the past year.

Selecting a Broker to Represent You

19

You are liquidating your largest asset.

You need to pick someone who is organized and experienced—someone you can trust. Your broker will be advising you on what to fix and will help you set the sales price and commissions. They will be creating a marketing strategy, coordinating showings, holding open houses, negotiating with buyer's agents, inspectors and appraisers and coordinating with the lender, title company and escrow closer. Organization is key!

Weak, lazy or incompetent broker syndrome

You've seen their listings and have clicked right by without a second thought. The photos have bad lighting and the house feels like a cave because they took the pictures themselves with their smart phone! The toilet seat is up. The house is messy and cluttered. The listing is over-priced. It languishes on the market, and after twenty to thirty days, we start seeing price reductions.

Ask about experience, background, and results.

How many sellers have they represented in the last year? Do their listings sell quickly with multiple offers or do they linger and require price reductions? Ask the broker if they have a secret superpower. For example, my background in construction and accounting helps me make sound recommendations for repairs, and my past life as a professional organizer helps me keep everything running smoothly.

Ask about your home's negative features.

No home is perfect. It is important to recognize what drawbacks your home may have, and then ask the broker what their plan would be to handle these. (See Chapter 6.) You need someone who can give you expert advice, help you neutralize negatives and develop a plan and timeline to get your home ready to sell.

Ask for and call their references.

Get references for three recent listing clients and take the time to call them. Ask the clients if they were happy with the broker's service. Was the broker responsive and easy to reach? Did they have exceptional negotiating skills? Were they organized? Did the client receive good advice and feel supported throughout the process?

Your house MUST look good online!

People decide if they will go look at your home within a couple of seconds of viewing it online, so it is imperative that your house looks beautiful online. Staging and photography are so important that I have devoted three chapters to this subject. Note that experience does not equal good results. Some of the worst listings come from brokers with thirty-plus years of experience.

25

Look at the broker's other listings.

This is The One Thing that you can do to make sure you get a good broker: ask them to show you their current, pending and past sales. Are the homes staged? Do they look beautiful? Homes that look beautiful online and in person sell faster and for higher prices. Would you pick those homes to go view, or would you just click past and say, "Next"?

How will they market your home?

The most important part of marketing your home is having it look beautiful online and in person. Next, ask your broker about Internet marketing and if they do open houses, which can be a great way to get a large number of people through your home quickly. Ask to see some of their flyers and other printed materials so you can check the quality.

Do you "click" with the broker?

Once you have determined they have the necessary skills, you need to determine if you connect with them. Are they patient and ready to explain things to you? Do they care about you personally and have a "heart to serve"? Selling your house and moving is stressful. You need someone who is sensitive to your needs and family situation, who will help minimize the stress—not just tell you how great they are!

Should I hire a discount firm?

A discount on real estate commissions may sound very appealing. The question is, what are you giving up to get the discount? What is the quality level of the brokers who are willing to forgo their commissions? Will they be able to advise you on how to maximize the sale of your home? Be sure to read the shocking story in the Introduction of this book where one seller lost $100K to save $10,650 in commissions.

Getting Your Home Ready to Sell

29

Ideally three months before you list

Interview real estate brokers using the process in Chapter 2. If you select carefully, your broker should be able to give you expert guidance that is specific to your home, including what repairs to make, what to clean, which furniture to keep and what to move out.

30

Fix it up or sell as-is?

Do you have the time and resources to do the work to maximize the return on your property, or do your circumstances require a quick sale in as-is condition? Putting some time, effort and money into improving your home before listing it can increase your bottom line drastically, but not everyone has the circumstances to do this. Be realistic about what you can actually do.

31

Approximately 80% can't visualize completed repairs!

For those of us who can visualize a home differently from its current condition, it is hard to understand that the majority of buyers simply can't picture what the home will be like AFTER. It is imperative to make the home look as beautiful as possible so it will appeal to the most buyers in order to get the highest price possible.

The initial consultation with your broker

When doing an initial walk-through, I am looking for the potential in the home, how I can best market it and what staging needs to be done. I will make recommendations on repairs, talk with you about how much time you realistically need to get ready, and together we will make an Action Plan.

33

Identifying potential and maximizing the results

I always look for the potential that is hiding in a home and ask, "What can we do to maximize this potential?" For example, if there are only two bedrooms, perhaps we could add a closet to the den and market it as a three-bedroom home. Is there potential for a mother-in-law suite? Do you have an exceptional yard or zoning for a home-based business?

Multiple offers—achieving the Holy Grail

Every seller wants a bidding war on their home. In order to achieve this, there are definite steps to be taken by you and your broker, and it all starts with the Action Plan. All of the recommendations in this book are designed to work toward getting multiple offers. While it would be exciting to have twenty offers on your house, it only takes two to start a bidding war!

35

Pricing strategy to get multiple offers

To generate a bidding war, the price MUST be set below market value. This is often the hardest part for a seller. It takes guts to price your home $10,000 to $25,000 low! Also, it is best for the price to be set at a round number in $25,000 increments, as this is how buyers search. For example, if you set the price at $549,950, you will miss buyers searching with a minimum of $550,000.

36

Have a home inspection done first.

Your buyer will most likely be conducting a home inspection. Wouldn't it be great to know in advance what the home inspector will find? By having your home pre-inspected, you will have the in-depth knowledge needed to prioritize repairs. Plus, you will not be blindsided by a larger repair or shocked to find that you have rodents in your crawl space!

Which repairs net the greatest return?

First, do the basics. For the home to be financeable for the largest number of buyers possible, including FHA and VA buyers, the most important repairs are a sound roof, fixing safety issues and no peeling paint. The next priority is to fix obvious problems that may scare buyers away (plumbing or electrical problems) and make sure all your systems are in working order.

Individualism versus appealing to the masses

Our homes are special to us because they are a reflection of who we are. However, you want the buyer to be able to picture themselves living there, so you will need to depersonalize and make the house as neutral as possible. Neutral colors make your home look larger and will have the broadest appeal. Painting over bright or dark colors is always a good idea.

Ideal versus doable— let's be realistic.

Having your home in perfect condition before it goes on the market would be ideal, but we live in the real world. You may not be in a position to put on that new roof. You may have a child with special needs or work sixty to seventy hours a week. It's O.K. Work with your broker to prioritize the items that will make the biggest impact. Do what you can and don't stress about the rest. ☺

Staging to Increase Your Bottom Line

40

Take a lesson from the pros.

New home builders and professional home flippers spend thousands of dollars staging their houses because they know that they will get a large return for every dollar spent in staging. They are in the real estate business for one reason—to make money. Take a lesson from the pros and stage your house!

How much more might I make?

The National Association of Realtors says that you can expect to net one to five percent more by staging your house, and for every $1,000 invested in staging you can expect to gain $4,000 or more. One of my sellers spent $3,000 on repairs and staging, and sold for $39,000 more.

42

Staging companies don't like your cat.

Most staging companies in the greater Seattle area only stage vacant homes and will not bring their inventory into a home that is occupied, especially if there are kids and pets in the home. You can usually book a consultation with the stager for an hour or two to give you advice, or your broker may be like me and do their own staging or be able to recommend the two or three staging companies that still do occupied homes.

The niche of staging occupied homes

Since very few staging companies work in occupied homes, out of necessity, I started doing the staging myself, to work with sellers to use the furnishings they already have and then bring my own items in to make the home really shine. Filling this niche gives me the power to maximize the potential in every listing. Plus, it gives me the flexibility to help sellers by allowing them to pay for my staging at closing, if necessary.

44

How much will staging cost me?

If the house is empty, plan to spend about $1,800 for a two-bedroom condo and $3,000 to $4000 for a four-bedroom house. This is an out-of-pocket cost that you will need to pay up front. If the home is occupied, staging costs will vary greatly depending on how many of your current furnishings can be used, and I will give you a quote for the cost. Refer back to Lesson 40 if you feel uncertain about spending money up front!

Staging is not decorating or design.

The purpose of staging is to make your home appealing to the largest number of buyers. While interior design needs to be functional and beautiful, staging only has to look good for a short period of time. For example, the living room does not need a TV, and to make the rooms look larger, I don't put dressers in bedrooms, and most people don't even notice!

Include a theme when planning staging.

When making a plan for staging, I start by thinking about the demographic of the most likely buyer for the house, and then plan the staging to appeal to that demographic. For example, for a two-bedroom condo on the third floor, the most likely buyer may be a single person or perhaps a couple in their mid-thirties or forties. So, the staging theme might be "smart, sophisticated urban living."

Staging to get maximum emotional impact

The psychology of sales tells us that emotions motivate people to buy, so every part of staging needs to work toward creating a positive emotional response in the buyer. We want to create a response of "WOW! This home is BEAUTIFUL! I can picture myself living here" when they walk in the front door. When I stage, I always consider what the psychological impact will be on the buyer.

Neutralizing Negatives or Converting to Positives

Identifying problem areas in your home

A big part of staging is distracting the eye from problem areas. When doing the initial planning walk-through, I am looking at the house through the critical eye of a potential buyer to try and spot their objections in advance. Like any good sales presentation, if we can eliminate buyer objections in advance, we will be ahead of the game!

Feature cards to highlight the positives

One of my favorite tools is feature cards which highlight upgrades and areas of potential in your home. I call these my "silent salesmen," since they sell your home when I am not there. They are designed to focus the buyer's attention on your home's best qualities and subconsciously build value in their mind.

50

Feature cards to neutralize the negatives

Is the condo located in a gated community because the crime rate in the area is high? To neutralize this, I would put a feature card near the entryway that says, "Feel Secure in the Gated Community." Does the property back up to the freeway? The card would read, "Location is a Commuter's Dream with Quick and Easy Access to I-5."

51

Custom solutions needed for problem areas

I love the challenge of coming up with a staging solution for the funky house that has some odd or "interesting" feature. Each situation is unique, requiring a creative solution specifically designed for that particular home. The next few lessons are examples of how I neutralized problem areas in recent listings, with website links to before and after photos.

52

You don't have a dining room?

In this condo, I created a dining area by pushing the couch farther down in the living room to free up space closer to the kitchen. I then created a cozy and romantic dining space using a small, bar-height table with a feature card saying, "Enjoy a Romantic Dinner for Two! Plus, there is plenty of space for a larger table." Go to ThePelhamGroupNW.com/dining for pictures.

53

Balcony with a parking lot view

This balcony had an ugly view but the southern exposure was perfect for container gardening. So, I staged the balcony with a small "potting bench" complete with pots, a bag of potting soil and a spade. A feature card saying, "Balcony with Southern Exposure is Perfect for Container Gardening" anchored the idea in the buyer's mind. See ThePelhamGroupNW.com/balcony.

54

The light-to-extreme fixer-upper

I had a listing that was in foreclosure. It needed a new roof, windows, flooring and electrical panel, and had rodents in the crawl space. The seller did not have any financial resources, but he was able to get friends to help him paint and clean. I then staged it to the max and generated a bidding war. We got nineteen offers and sold for $25,000 over list price. See ThePelhamGroupNW.com/fixer.

55

Don't cover up defects or damage.

When staging, you can't legally hide defects or damage. If you put a rug on a hardwood floor that needs to be refinished, be sure to disclose the floor's damage when filling out the Form 17 Seller's Property Disclosure. The point of staging is to distract from the defects—not hide them—and show how potentially beautiful the property could be. To protect yourself legally, be sure to disclose all known defects on the Form 17.

56

Offer buyers a home warranty plan.

A home warranty is a type of insurance plan that offers protection against unexpected repairs in your home's systems and appliances. The cost runs around $285 to $500, which is paid from the proceeds of the sale at closing. By offering this, you help remove some of the buyer's concerns. Plus, depending on the plan, you may also be covered during the time the house is listed.

57

Would virtual staging work for me?

Virtual staging is a new process where furnishings are digitally inserted into photos of the house. Cost is $32 to $69 per photo. The resulting photos can be a good way to generate showings, but of course, virtual staging does nothing to neutralize negatives or distract the eye from defects. I do not recommend this because it can be a real letdown for a buyer to walk into an empty house.

58

Even beautiful homes may need editing.

While your home may be beautiful, up-to-date and in great repair, it still needs to be presented to the public in the best possible light so it will appeal to the largest number of people. Follow the advice in the Top 10 Pointers in the next chapter. Your broker should help you set priorities and give suggestions on specific refinements and edits.

My Top 10 Pointers for Staging

59

A plan to depersonalize your house

In general, you want to remove personal items like family photos, mementos and collections. Get your teenager to remove posters from their walls. Pack up religious, political, or any potential controversial items and anything that could distract the buyer's attention from your home. Remember that we are aiming to make your home feel neutral so that it appeals to the largest number of buyers.

60

Give them a good first impression.

Buyers will often drive by first to determine if they want to view the property with their broker. Step back and look at the front of your house with a critical eye. What will stand out first to the buyer? Freshen up the landscaping and the paint (even if it's just painting the front door). Power wash the driveway and clean the windows. Curb appeal is important!

61

Remove at least half your stuff.

It's time to start moving! To make your home look larger, cleaner, in better repair, and to have great photos, I recommend packing up at least half of your belongings. This is a great time to sort out things you no longer use, have a garage sale or donate to charity. If necessary, you can stack boxes neatly in the garage, or better yet, rent a storage unit.

Neat and clean equals good maintenance.

Buyers will pay more money for a home that it is exceptionally well-maintained. Subconsciously, we perceive that a home that is neat and clean must also have had good maintenance. Invest the time and/or money to deep clean your house. Clean the baseboards and the windows and have the carpet cleaned. Tidy up the electronics and cords. The neater your house is, the less your buyer will question your home's maintenance.

63

Got old furniture? Use accent pillows!

Invest $200 to $300 in accent pillows for a complete new look for your living room and bedroom. Pick a color theme that works with your existing furnishings. Look for pillows in that color at HomeGoods, TJ Maxx and Ross for around $15 to $25 for sets of two. Then create impact by adding a few embellished or elegant pillows at $35 to $45. See ThePelhamGroupNW.com/pillows.

Kitchen should feel luxurious not laborious!

There should be no sign that work actually happens in this kitchen! First, clear EVERYTHING off the counters. To make it easier to live in the staged kitchen, I like to create vignettes of items on trays which can easily be moved when it's time to cook dinner. My go-to kitchen trays include an Italian-themed, high-end pasta tray and a French press coffee tray. See ThePelhamGroupNW.com/trays.

Master bedroom retreat/master bathroom spa

Create a master suite that feels like a private oasis. Use bedding with a bold but elegant pattern and add accent pillows in a restful color like blue or green. Carry this color into the bath with new, fluffy towels, a few elegant accents on the counter, and some white orchids. Complete the retreat with a tea-for-two tray on the bed and soft music. See ThePelhamGroupNW.com/master.

Bright and bold artwork creates focus.

Stand in the doorway. Where does your eye naturally go? What will be the camera's focus? Add bright and bold canvas artwork on that wall to give each photo a focal point. Art with glass is not as good, since the glass will reflect the camera's flash. My favorite sources for inexpensive canvas pictures are Ross, TJ Maxx, HomeGoods, Amazon and Kohls online.
See ThePelhamGroupNW.com/artwork.

67

Improve lighting and open all blinds.

A quick and easy update for older recessed can lighting is to install LED trims (cost is about $8 to $12 each). Simply remove the old bulb and screw in the new trim bulb and the old light fixture looks new and modern! Bring in more lamps to improve poorly lit rooms. The photographer will want the blinds open and all the lights turned on, and you should do this for every open house and showing.

Tips to deal with unpleasant odors

We get used to the smells in our own homes. Ask a friend to stop by and do a smell test. While your home is on the market, refrain from cooking foods with strong odors like curry, fish, and hard-boiled eggs. Clean the cat box regularly. Ozone air purifiers (which can be rented at an equipment rental store) reduce persistent odors. Be sure to run it when you are not at home, as it can cause headaches.

Just Before and First Week Listed

Minimizing stress with my listing plan.

Selling your house and having to move is one of life's most stressful events, and the listing week is full of activity which can be stressful. My carefully planned and scheduled listing and sales process is designed to minimize the stress on you and your family.

Staging items brought into the home

If you are living in the home, I like to bring the staging items in on Monday or Tuesday of the listing week when possible. This gives you the maximum time to get the home ready and minimizes the time that you have to live with staging. Please make sure that the house is clean and you are ready for the staging.

Tips for living in staged homes

Use a basket or a caddy to stash daily-use bathroom items under the sink. Since you can't use the staging towels, run your wet towels through the dryer after you shower. Beds must be made every morning. Rinse dishes after use and put them immediately into the dishwasher. Keep prescriptions, firearms, bills and other personal documents locked away.

Professional photography is the next step.

The photographer will want all the lights turned on and the curtains and blinds opened. Photography generally takes about one to two hours. I use a photographer who digitally adds blue skies, greens up the grass, and adds fire in the fireplace. Photos usually are back within one to two days.

Marketing materials are now in production.

Once the photos are received, the flyer can be completed and sent to the printer. I have my flyers professionally printed, full bleed, on heavy gloss paper to increase the aura of luxury. The photos are uploaded to the Multiple Listing Service (MLS) website, and we are ready to go live either Thursday night or sometime on Friday. The listing is then syndicated to hundreds of real estate websites.

74

Packing up the dog and kids

Once we are live, showings can start right away. To get the best results, we want to make it as easy as possible to show the house. In my experience, the people who book showings on Thursday or Friday night after work often make offers, so be ready with a plan to get out of the house quickly. Put your pet in a crate if you can't take it with you.

Plan a weekend getaway if possible.

I recommend that you plan a little trip for the weekend. By now, you will need a break, and this is the perfect time for a trip. My sales process is designed to get the maximum number of people through your home while limiting the stress on you, and I recommend that you plan to be gone as much as possible Friday through Sunday.

Open houses scheduled Saturday and Sunday

Scheduling an open house on both Saturday and Sunday is the most efficient way to get a lot of buyers through your house in a short period of time. Plus, it gives me the opportunity to really sell the home's features directly to the buyers since many brokers send their buyers out by themselves to look at open houses on the weekends.

Opinion on setting offer review dates

The MLS gives us the option to "Review Offers Upon Receipt" or to set an offer review date. Generally, I recommend not setting a review date until we have at least two offers in hand. Setting a review date up-front can scare off buyers who are tired of losing bidding wars. Buyer fatigue is a real problem in a hot market.

Bidding war only needs two offers.

I almost always recommend that we wait until after the Open Houses are finished before reviewing offers. If we end up with multiple offers, I will assist you in evaluating the strengths of each offer. If appropriate, I will use professional negotiating strategies to increase the price of your home and/or get better terms.

Highest offer is not always best.

When evaluating offers, many things need to be considered. I call the buyer's loan officer and ask specific questions about their financial situation and the loan type and terms. Some buyers may have done a pre-inspection or may waive contingencies. Or, perhaps having a few days after closing to move may be important to you. We will weigh all these factors when making a decision on which offer to accept.

Sale Timeline One: Pending through Appraisal

80

You are under contract! Now what?

Once both parties have agreed on the terms and the Purchase and Sale Agreement has been signed by all, we now have Mutual Acceptance and your house is changed to "Pending" in the MLS. The Mutual Acceptance Date is important, as it is the basis for various contingencies.

81

Don't remove staging and feature cards!

Resist the temptation to remove the feature cards and staging for two reasons: 1. The sale may fail for various reasons, and you don't want to have to re-stage the home. 2. We want to present the house in the best possible light to the appraiser, as this will help us get the highest appraised value for the house.

Getting the earnest money to escrow

The buyer is required to deliver the earnest money to the escrow company or to the buyer's broker within two days of Mutual Acceptance. If they deliver it to their broker, the broker then has three days to deliver it to escrow. The escrow company serves as a neutral third party that holds the earnest money until closing.

Ordering the Resale Certificate (condos only)

For condos, you will need to order a Resale Certificate from your property management company. The Resale Certificate provides critical financial information to the buyer and the lender regarding the Home Owners Association. Order and pay for this immediately, as management companies often take the full ten-day standard time period. You will need to pay for this up front, usually about $250 to $350.

84

General information on home inspection contingency

If the buyer included an inspection period, your broker will coordinate the home inspection appointment with you. The buyer's broker will be present with the inspector and the buyers may also attend the inspection. It is preferred that you are not at home and that you either take pets with you or crate them during the inspection.

They can remove my toilet—seriously??

The home inspection may include the right to do a sewer scope. A plumbing company will feed a camera through the sewer line out to the street to check for issues. Occasionally, they may need to remove the toilet to get the camera into the sewer line. Once they are done, the plumber will replace the wax ring and re-install the toilet.

Septic system pumping and well tests

Occasionally, septic systems can still be found in the city, but generally are located in more rural areas. Septic systems must be pumped and inspected as part of the sales process, and well water is usually tested. The seller pays for the septic inspection and pumping and the buyer usually pays for the well test.

What happens after the inspection's done?

The buyer's broker will send an Inspection Response form. The possible results from the inspection are: they accept the house as-is, they request repairs or a price reduction or they cancel. Your response choices are: accept their requests for repairs or price reduction, counter offer or cancel the sale. Further negotiations may need to be made, and your broker will guide you through this process.

Why do you need title insurance?

The title company will search county records for any liens against the buyer, the seller and the property, and for easements, undisclosed heirs, errors or fraud. The Title Policy guarantees that you have the right to sell the property and that the buyer will receive a clear title.

Why does title need your SSN?

The title company needs to check for marriages, divorces, bankruptcies, judgements, tax liens, or things like past-due child support. These items may affect the marketability of the title or may need to be paid before or at the time of closing. Title will also get a payoff amount from your mortgage company.

90

Who pays for the title insurance?

Generally, two title insurance policies are issued. The Owner's Policy guarantees that seller is providing clear title to the buyer. This is a seller cost and will have been included in the estimated closing costs provided to you by your broker when you listed the house. The second policy protects the lender and is paid by the buyer as part of their loan costs.

– 91 –

Getting ready for the appraisal inspection

Once the home inspection has been resolved, the appraisal is ordered by the lender. Your broker will coordinate the date and time. Prepare as if you were having another open house. Staging and feature cards should be in place. Also, earthquake straps on the hot water heater and carbon monoxide and smoke detectors are required by law.

92

What if the appraisal is low?

In a market where prices are appreciating quickly, appraisals often come in low. If that happens with your house, your broker should check for rare mathematical or procedural errors. The options are: order a new appraisal, lower the price, negotiate a compromise or reject the appraisal. Holding the deal together at this point requires experience and expert guidance from your broker.

Sale Timeline Two: the Last Week

When is the final walk-through?

The final walk-through should be three to five days before closing to confirm that any repairs agreed to in the Inspection Response have been completed, that all appliances and home systems such as heating and plumbing are in the same functioning state as when the offer was made, and all items that were stated to be included in the sale are still present in the home.

94

When do you move everything out?

Unless a delayed possession was negotiated at the start, all of your belongings need to be moved out of the home before the closing date. Sometimes there are delays from the lender which may cause the closing date to be postponed, so check with your broker to make sure the sale is on track to close on time BEFORE you schedule your moving date.

95

Requirements for cleaning at move-out

The contract states, "Seller shall clean the interiors of any structures and remove all trash, debris and rubbish from the Property prior to the Buyer taking possession." Please plan for this when you finish moving. If you do not clean the property, it can cost $500 to $800 or more to hire a cleaning or junk removal company.

Closing disclosure will arrive from escrow.

The escrow company gathers all the documents from the lender, the mortgage lienholder(s), the real estate brokers and the title company and prepares the Closing Disclosure (CD). The Closing Disclosure is sent to the brokers for them to double check for accuracy. It is then sent to the Buyer and the Seller. Please look this over carefully and ask any questions you might have.

Scheduling the signing of the documents

The escrow company will contact both the Seller and Buyer to sign separately. They may give you an option to schedule the signing at either their office or at a remote location such as your home or office. Please note that remote signing usually has an additional fee of approximately $75 to $150 which will be included in the costs shown on your Closing Disclosure. Allow about 45 minutes to an hour for the signing.

Closing happens a few days later.

Usually, funding, recording and closing happen at least one or two days after you sign. When the buyer's funds have been received by escrow, they will then send the transaction to the county for recording. Usually near the end of the day, the county sends recording numbers back to escrow, and the sale is complete!

99

Transferring the keys to the buyer

Per standard MLS contract (unless modified), the transfer of ownership happens at 9 p.m. on the day of closing. Your broker will make arrangements to get the keys to the buyer's broker, who will give them to the buyer. Be sure to leave any extra keys and the garage door remotes on the kitchen counter.

100

When do you get your money?

Generally, you will receive the funds the day after the sale records with the county. The escrow company will transfer the proceeds of the sale in the manner that you arranged with them, usually either wire transfer directly to your bank account or cashier's check. Congratulations! All your hard work has paid off and you made it to the finish line!

Acknowledgments

Thanks are owed to the following people:

- To Braden Gustafson, Senior Appraiser with Gustafson & Associates, for weighing in on the value of a parking space and for information on the difficulty of measuring the value of waterfront and views.

- To Katrina Eileen Romatowski for insights into zoning issues and her huge vision for our brokerage.

- To Mitchell Pelham and Lisa Forret for assisting with research and statistics when I got stuck.

- To Ella Porras, my personal assistant and transaction coordinator, for all her support and hard work in creating and maintaining the web pages for the bonus material and photos.

- To Sarah Vanausdoll and Will Flanagan—the dynamic duo of photography who are responsible for the cover photo and all the real estate photos in the online bonus materials.

- To Brien Pelham for all his encouragement and for his help with the final edit and reorganization.

Word of mouth is crucial for any author or real estate broker to succeed. If you enjoyed this book, please consider leaving a review on Amazon.com, even if it is only a line or two. It would make all the difference, and I would appreciate it very much.

Please contact me with any questions or comments:

Kim Pelham
Real Estate Broker with
Katrina Eileen
701 Fifth Avenue, Suite 4200
Seattle, Washington 98104
Email: Kim@ThePelhamGroupNW.com
ThePelhamGroupNW.com
Mobile: 425-213-8761

The Pelham Group

KATRINA EILEEN

BROKERS KE INVESTORS

A Note from Katrina About Washington State's First Social Purpose Corporation for Real Estate:

When one's drive for purpose drives one's endeavor for profit, Good Happens.

In everything we do, we ask ourselves, "Is this life affirming? Does this create something self-sustaining?" If the answer is, "Yes." then we are all in.

Katrina Eileen is a social purpose corporation whose mission affirms the first of the United Nations' 2030 Sustainable Development goals—to eliminate poverty. We are adding our verse to this song.

We will do this in two ways: by providing affordable housing and by teaching real estate entrepreneurship. We believe that owning the dirt under your feet and the roof over your head is a possibility that provides a profound sense of security and financial freedom. Property ownership creates wealth not just for the individual, but for each generation to come.

The wealthy among us have stored wealth in land since the time that land ownership for the individual was first possible. Throughout history, land ownership has been a hedge against inflation and has assured the transfer of wealth from she who earned it to her heirs.

Creating wealth through property acquisition isn't difficult, but the know-how and confidence to act aren't shared equally in our community. At *Katrina Eileen*, it is our mission to help end poverty by providing affordable housing and by teaching those with an interest in learning how one might create a legacy of abundance through the vehicle of real property ownership.

Katrina Eileen Romatowski
Designated Broker

About the *Six-Word Lessons Series*

Legend has it that Ernest Hemingway was challenged to write a story using only six words. He responded with the story, "For sale: baby shoes, never worn." The story tickles the imagination. Why were the shoes never worn? The answers are left up to the reader's imagination.

This style of writing has a number of aliases: postcard fiction, flash fiction, and micro fiction. Lonnie Pacelli was introduced to this concept in 2009 by a friend, and started thinking about how this extreme brevity could apply to today's communication culture of text messages, tweets and Facebook posts. He wrote the first book, *Six-Word Lessons for Project Managers*, then started helping other authors write and publish their own books in the series.

The books all have six-word chapters with six-word lesson titles, each followed by a one-page description. They can be written by entrepreneurs who want to promote their businesses, or anyone with a message to share.

See the entire *Six-Word Lessons Series* at **6wordlessons.com**